BATS

CONTENTS

Written by Anne Gordon

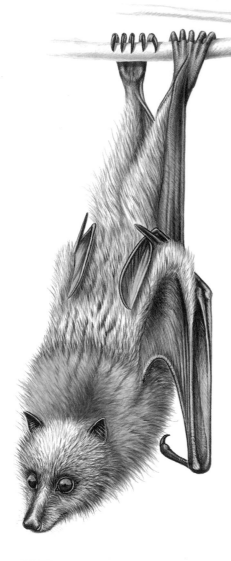

What Are Bats?

Bats can fly, but they are not birds. Bats belong to the group of animals called *Mammals*. Many different kinds of animals are mammals, including creatures as different from one another as whales, mice, gorillas, and horses. Human beings are also mammals.

A gray-headed flying fox from Australia is a kind of bat. Like all other kinds of bats, it belongs to the group of animals called mammals.

What Are Mammals?

Mammals have special features that make them different from other groups of animals, such as birds and reptiles. Mammals are warm-blooded. The babies are born live and mammals feed their babies on milk. Mammals have fur or hair covering their bodies. They have teeth. Mammals also have ears on the outside of their heads.

Bats have all these *mammalian* features.

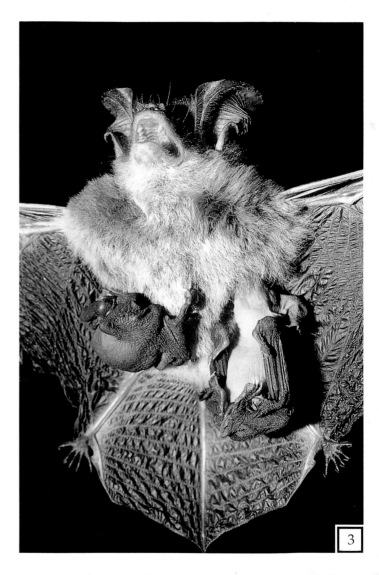

A Gould's long-eared bat (Australia) suckles her young twins. Like other mammals, bats feed their babies on milk.

3

Bats Are Special

Bats can do one thing that no other mammals can do. Bats can fly.

The structure of a bat's wing is very similar to that of a human arm and hand. It has an upper arm, an elbow, a long forearm, and a wrist. The bat's "thumb" is a claw at the top of the wing. The long "fingers" form the framework of the wing itself.

The wing is covered with skin, which is very tough and flexible. This skin is covered with tiny transparent hairs. In many bats, the skin spreads out from the bottom of the wing to join the feet and tail.

A horseshoe bat in flight, clearly showing the structure of a bat's wing.

4

A vampire bat hopping along the ground. Most bats move very awkwardly except when they are flying, but a vampire bat can walk, hop, and run.

Different Kinds of Bats

There are nearly 1000 different species of bats. Bats are found almost everywhere in the world, except in the Antarctic and in the colder areas above the Arctic Circle.

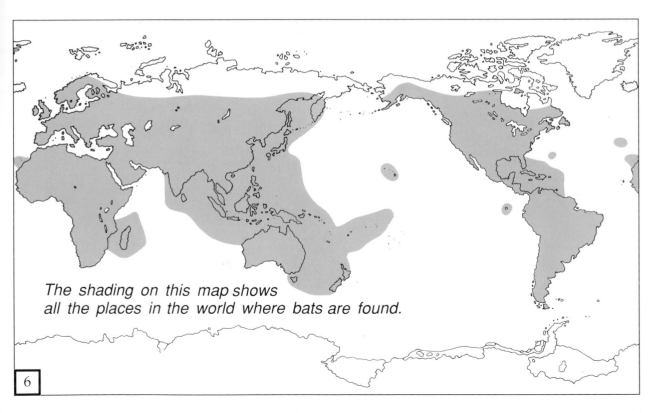

The shading on this map shows all the places in the world where bats are found.

The Gambian epauletted fruit bat has large eyes and excellent eyesight.

The tent-building bat and the wrinkled-faced bat have unusual nose-leaves.

Different species of bats can have a wide variety of body features. For example, all bats have ears, but these come in many sizes and shapes. Many ears have a small flap which covers the ear opening; this is called a tragus.

All bats also have eyes. However, the size and shape of bats' eyes vary from one species to another, and some species of bats have much better eyesight than others.

Bats have very unusual noses. Some bats have a strange shape around their noses and nostrils. This is called a nose-leaf, and it can be many different shapes.

The enormous nose of the hammer-headed bat is used to make loud cries.

The sword-nosed bat is named after the shape of its unusual nose-leaf.

Most bats have tails, which help them steer when they are flying, but not all bats' tails are the same. Some tails are joined to the back legs with thin skin, making them like a wing. Other tails poke out a long way past this skin. Some bats have *no* tail.

The mouse-tailed bat has a tail that is not joined to the wings and legs with skin. The long tail hangs down during flight.

Most bats have dull-colored brown or gray fur, but some have brighter color patterns. The different colorings depend on what bats eat and where they live.

Some bats have brightly colored fur. These illustrations show the yellow-winged false vampire bat (left), the vespertilionid spotted bat (middle), and the orange horseshoe bat (right).

What Do Bats Eat?

Some bats eat only fruit; these bats have strong teeth and jaws for chewing. Other bats eat flowers; these bats have long noses and rough tongues to reach nectar and pollen.

The spear-nosed long-tongued bat can hover like a hummingbird while it sips nectar with its long tongue.

The Barbados fruit bat from the West Indies.

Many bat species eat mainly insects. Most of these bats capture insects during flight, either pushing a flying insect toward their mouths with a wing, or using their tails as a kind of scoop to catch the insect. Some bats pick up insects from leaves or from the ground. Bats may eat small insects while flying, but they will carry larger insects to a nearby perch to eat them.

Many bats have a mixed diet, eating fruit and insects.

A long-eared bat searching for insects.

A few bats are carnivorous. This means that they eat other animals such as frogs and lizards. They hang in trees while waiting for passing prey.

After spotting its prey, a bat will swoop and capture the animal, killing it with a bite to the head and neck. Some carnivorous bats even catch other bats during flight.

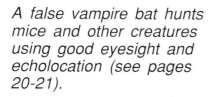

A false vampire bat hunts mice and other creatures using good eyesight and echolocation (see pages 20-21).

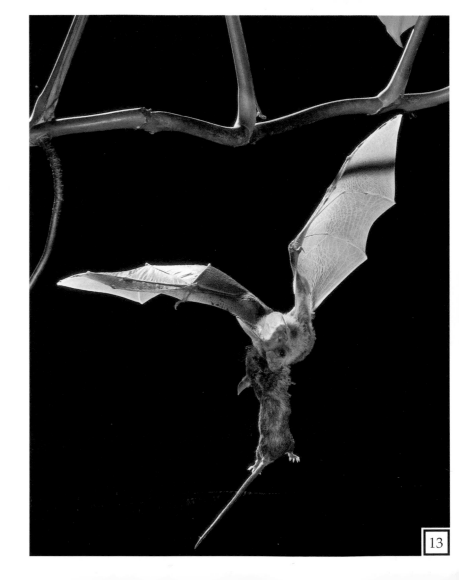

Bulldog or fisherman bats skim insects and fish from water. To do this they have special feet, which are long and pointed like a rake. These bats are found in the tropical areas of Central and South America.

A bulldog or fisherman bat raking the water for a fish, which it will grab in its long sharp claws.

Vampire bats live exclusively on the blood of other animals. They use their pointed, razor-sharp teeth for making a small wound in another animal, and then they lap up the blood with their tongues.

A vampire bat has pointed teeth.

A vampire bat lapping blood from the foot of a chicken.

Where Do Bats Live?

During the day, most bats roost by hanging upside down. Some hang in trees among the leaves. Others prefer darker places such as caves, rock crevices, and hollow trees.

A California leaf-nosed bat roosting upside down, with its wings folded at the sides of its body.

There may be as many as 40 million Mexican free-tailed bats in this cave.

Bats' caves often provide excellent nurseries, with the bats grouping together to have their babies and look after them. The very young babies will be left together in a cave, while the mothers go out for food.

A nursery cave of mouse-eared bats. Even among so many babies, the mothers and their young can find each other, using a special call, and perhaps a special smell.

Some bats make shelters for themselves in naturally curling leaves, where they roost in small groups.

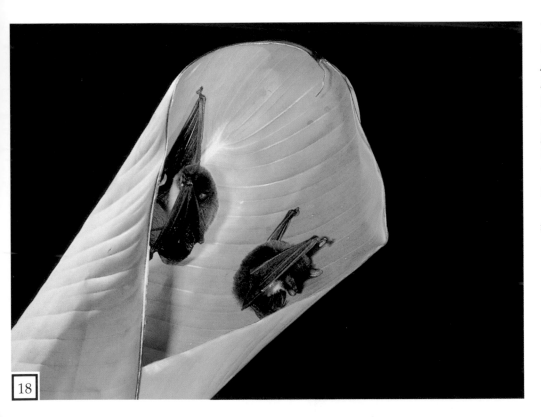

Tiny disk-winged bats of Central and South America roosting inside banana leaves. They have a sucker on each thumb and foot which grips the leaf. They roost with their heads upward, which is an unusual position for bats.

Some tent-building bats make a shelter by cutting the ribs of a leaf to make it curl up. Several bats will roost in this specially made *tent*.

Tiny Honduran tent bats roosting in the leaf tent they have made. They are one of the few kinds of bats that are white.

Bats' Senses

Many bats have poor eyesight, but they are able to hunt and catch tiny insects at night. They do this by using their voices and ears in a special way, called *echolocation*.

The bat sends out sounds from its mouth, or from its nose if it has a nose-leaf. These sounds spread outward from the bat's head like ripples in a pond. If there is an insect nearby, the sounds bounce off the insect and come back to the bat. The bat's ears can pick up this echo and tell exactly where the insect is.

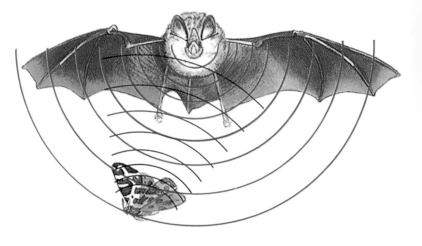

As a bat flies toward an insect, it keeps sending out sounds, and the echoes coming back change as the insect comes closer and closer. This is called echolocation.

A horseshoe bat, named because of the shape of its nose-leaf, has poor eyesight. This bat is chasing a moth in the dark using echolocation. Bats also use echolocation to steer their way around trees and other bats, and through caves.

Are Bats Evil?

Stories about bats often show them as evil, frightening creatures. But these stories are unfair. Perhaps humans have misunderstood bats' strange appearance and night-time habits. Bats are interesting and harmless creatures, which can help humans.

For example, many bats eat insects. They help to control the number of insects in the world. Other bats eat fruit and flowers. They do an important job in spreading seeds and pollen. This helps new plants to grow.

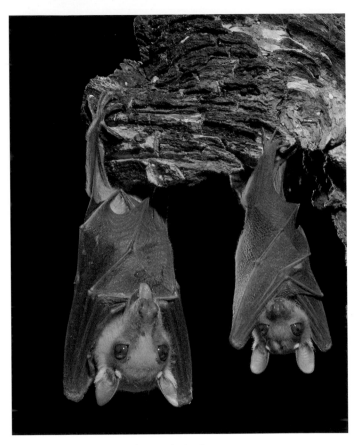

Wahlberg's epauletted fruit bats, like many other fruit bats, roost with their wings wrapped around their bodies. ◄

Conservation

Bats do not have any natural enemies, but humans often threaten their survival. For example, when humans clear forests for farms or houses, they often destroy the places where bats roost and find food. Sometimes bats do become a nuisance when they roost inside buildings. However, the answer is not to kill the bats; the bats will leave if the openings to the roosting place are blocked off. Humans can help bats by building roosting boxes in suitable places, such as trees, and by protecting the caves and other natural places where bats roost and find food.

Glossary

carnivorous — feeding on flesh or other animal matter

echolocation — a way of finding the position of things by sending out sound waves and listening for the echoes as they bounce back

mammal — warm-blooded animal whose babies are suckled on milk

mammalian — having the special features of mammals

roost — settle down for sleep

species — a group of animals or plants that have similar features

Index